THE SOUL JOURNAL

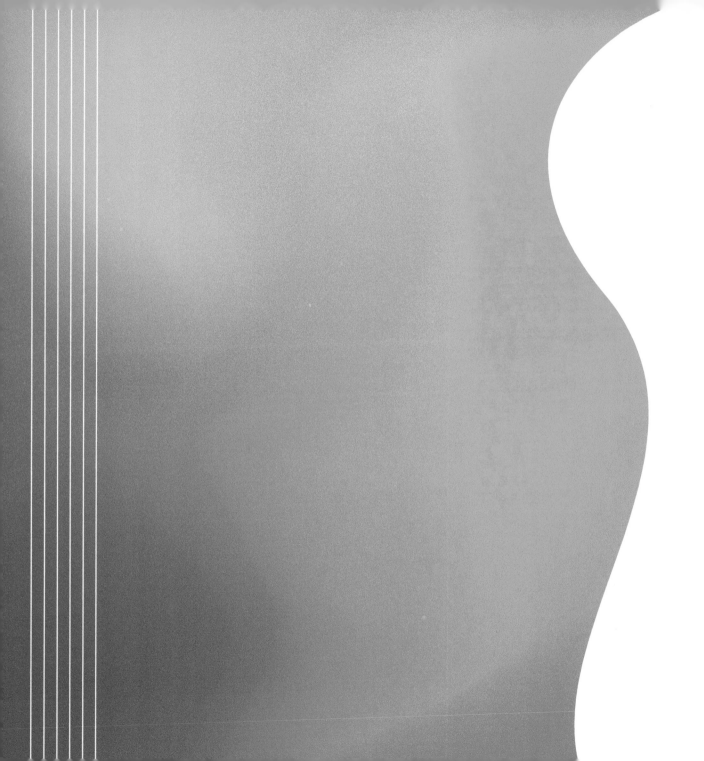

The
soul
JOURNAL

INSPIRING PROMPTS TO REFLECT, FIND INNER PEACE, AND NOURISH YOUR SPIRITUAL GROWTH

Sophia Godkin, PhD

**ROCKRIDGE
PRESS**

Interior and Cover Designer:
Brieanna H. Felschow
Art Producer: Samantha Ulban
Editor: Brian Sweeting
Production Editor: Holland Baker
Production Manager:
Martin Worthington

Illustrations by
Brieanna Hattey Felschow.
Author Photo Courtesy of Urban Gal
Photography, Marcela Bullen.

Paperback ISBN: 978-1-63878-121-9
R0

THIS JOURNAL BELONGS TO:

_____

INTRODUCTION

Welcome to *The Soul Journal*, your guided journey to connecting with, embracing, and living from everything that's true within you. My name is Dr. Sophia Godkin, and as a health psychologist and happiness and healing coach, I've helped people all over the world create a life that not only looks good on the outside but genuinely feels good on the inside, too. Like most people today, I grew up with a good understanding of how to build a life that looked good, yet I learned little about how to create one that felt good, too. And it's this experience that set me out on both a personal and professional quest to understand the building blocks of a truly joyful, meaningful, and authentic life.

For a period of more than ten years, I bounced between psychological, spiritual, relational, and energetic healing practices, adopting what felt good and what created positive transformation in myself and in my clients. After some time, it became clear to me that the techniques and practices that were truly healing and moving people toward a joyful, meaningful future all had one thing in common: They were helping people connect with their soul, from which qualities like compassion, courage, presence, and inner peace were able to be born.

It isn't enough to just read about creating an authentic, joyful, and meaningful life by connecting with our soul. We've got to invite ourselves into a process of self-discovery, self-understanding, self-expression, and self-love. That's exactly what the prompts and exercises in this journal will help you do.

In the context of this journal, "soul" refers to your true nature, true essence, true self, higher self, spirit, or any other set of words you might use to describe who you truly are (all of which will be used interchangeably throughout). In this journal, you will have boundless opportunities to explore, express, and experience this essence. You'll be invited to reflect on who you really are; uncover your true beliefs, desires, and values; actively understand and care for your emotional self; and connect and align with your inner knowing.

Consider this journal your trusted partner along your path to a more aligned and genuinely happy life. Like any good friend, this journal is here to listen to whatever's on your mind and in your heart, to provide support in a practical and compassionate way, and to ask tough questions when they might help you become more of who you were meant to be. Enjoy the journey! I know it will be a heart-opening, self-affirming, and soul-nourishing one.

HOW TO USE THIS JOURNAL

The prompts and exercises in this journal are designed to help you gain self-awareness, move gently past any resistance that arises, overcome conditioned fears, and apply what you've learned to replace old, limiting ways of thinking, doing, and being with new and supportive ones.

On each page, you'll find two prompts. The first "Reflect" prompt will ask you to take stock of a particular situation or feeling in your life to become aware of things as they are. The second "Center" prompt will ask you to tune in to who you *really* are and how you *want* to feel and be so that you can find greater alignment with your true self. These two prompts will be followed by a short exercise, titled "Act," which will encourage you to take steps to turn your feelings and reflections into practical actions.

Periodically, you will also find exercises, affirmations, and quotes designed to strengthen your connection with your true self. Repeat each affirmation out loud or in your mind as you visualize and internalize its message, and pause to contemplate the personal meaning and wisdom that each quote offers.

Work through the prompts in order or flip through the journal and complete whichever page speaks most to you on any given day. If a specific prompt or exercise resonates with you, expand on it or do it multiple times. If a prompt or exercise begins to feel like a lot, imagine a circle of people who are all using this book holding hands around you, offering kindness and reminding you that it's okay to feel what you feel. If something doesn't resonate, trust yourself to skip it or come back to it later. Let completing this journal itself be a process that's guided by your soul.

REFLECT: Do you respond more readily to the calling of your mind (which often comes in the form of thoughts) or your heart (which often comes in the form of gentle nudges and whispers)? How do you know?

CENTER: What is calling to your heart right now (e.g., a dream or goal to pursue, a training to take, a place to visit or live, etc.)? Write about it freely. Then think of a few words that capture how it feels to tune in to your heart's calling. Write those down, too.

ACT: Ask yourself, "What is one small step I can take to honor the calling of my heart more in my day-to-day life? And who or what can support me in making that happen?"

REFLECT: Would you say that you've been who you want to be in your life or that you've mostly been who the people around you want you to be? How so?

CENTER: What are the benefits of you being the person you want to be rather than the person others want you to be?

ACT: Starting with today, see if you can give yourself a little more permission to be who you want to be. Put less emphasis on what you "should" be doing or what you "have to" do and more on what makes you feel alive. What will you do differently today than you did yesterday?

REFLECT: What is *your* definition of success? A high-paying job? A life of love, inner peace, and joy? Financial freedom? An ability to honor your inner wisdom and disregard others' judgment and criticism? Something else? Describe what success means to you.

CENTER: Are any external pressures (from people or society) holding you back from pursuing *your* definition of success? What would it feel like to soften the need to meet all the external pressures and demands placed on you and step into your journey toward success as *you* define it?

ACT: With the pressure lessened, what can you now do that you weren't able to but wanted to do before? Write about it, identifying a first step you will take to begin shaping your life story into one based on *your* definition of success.

MY CHILDHOOD DREAMS

Think back to when you were between five and ten years old. Let yourself embody your essence at that age. From that embodied place, write or draw about your thoughts, feelings, dreams, and desires.

The best way
I can think of to
spend my time
is being
exactly
who I am meant
to be.

REFLECT: No matter whether something happened two days, two years, or two decades ago, we may still be holding on to it, especially if it caused us pain. Describe an old experience that you're holding on to.

CENTER: Being able to heal and move on from a past experience begins with being honest about it and feeling the feelings that remain as a result of it. Although it may be uncomfortable at first, how can opening up to the difficult feelings of your past hurts create room for present healing?

ACT: Find a safe and private space, bring to mind the hurtful experience that you've been holding on to, and give any difficult feelings permission to come up. Allow yourself to feel these feelings, reassuring yourself that they're a normal reaction to what you experienced. Then see if you can find kindness and compassion for your pain, like you would for another person going through this experience.

REFLECT: Be honest: Is it easy or difficult to accept the reality of a situation when it's not a situation you prefer?

CENTER: It can be tempting to protest against what's happening and argue with reality when it's not the way we want it to be. But accepting things exactly the way they are can be a path of inner peace and freedom. Why do you think it hurts so much to argue with reality? Do you think you'd feel any differently if you were more accepting of it?

Please keep in mind that "accepting the reality of a situation" doesn't mean you approve of what's happening; it means you acknowledge rather than fight the pain and can therefore focus on steps to cope with it.

ACT: Think of a part of your life where you're currently protesting the way things are by hoping they were radically different, blaming yourself or someone else for the way things are, or asserting that what's happening should never have happened. What would it mean to accept this reality with its related pain and/or shortcomings? What's one step you can take toward acceptance today?

MY PHYSICAL, EMOTIONAL, AND SPIRITUAL NEEDS

When you can meet your physical, emotional, and spiritual needs, life naturally progresses with joy and ease. When those needs are neglected, the opposite happens. Everything in life feels *more* effortful and burdensome. Put a check mark next to the physical, emotional, and spiritual needs that you personally have on a regular basis, and add any others that aren't already listed, keeping in mind that a need fulfilled in one category may also fulfill needs in another category.

PHYSICAL NEEDS

☐ Good night's sleep
☐ Fresh air
☐ Rest when needed
☐ Staying hydrated
☐ Mindful breathing
☐ Cuddles from a pet
☐ Healthy, balanced eating
☐ Sunlight
☐ Movement
☐ Sex and intimacy
☐ Safety
☐ ....
☐ ....
☐ ....
☐ ....
☐ ....
☐ ....
☐ ....

EMOTIONAL NEEDS

☐ Pleasure and fun
☐ Therapy
☐ Time for self-reflection
☐ Love and affection
☐ Silence
☐ Trust
☐ Kindness and compassion
☐ Healthy boundaries
☐ Feeling my feelings
☐ Managing stress
☐ Flexibility
☐ Doing something I love
☐ Independence
☐ Understanding
☐ ....
☐ ....
☐ ....

SPIRITUAL NEEDS

☐ Prayer
☐ Time for self-reflection
☐ Purpose
☐ Being charitable
☐ Acceptance
☐ Connection and belonging
☐ Stillness and mindfulness
☐ Forgiveness
☐ Creativity
☐ Time in nature
☐ Sacred space
☐ Permission to be me
☐ Growth
☐ Appreciating the little things
☐ Yoga
☐ ....
☐ ....

Anytime you're not feeling your best, come back to this page and ask yourself: "What do I need right now?" and "How can I create space in my life to meet this need?"

"Do you pay regular visits to yourself? Start now."

—RUMI

REFLECT: What have you focused on more intently in your life so far—your relationship with others or your relationship with yourself? If having a relationship with yourself is a new concept for you, you are not alone.

CENTER: In two or three words, describe what qualities you want your relationships with others to consistently include. How do you think the quality of your life would be different if all of your relationships, platonic and romantic, embodied these qualities?

ACT: Knowing that your relationship with yourself is a conduit of authentic connection with the people and things around you, what is one practical way that you can bring the qualities that you desire in your relationships with others into the relationship you have with yourself (e.g., I want others to truly understand me so I will spend some extra time listening to and understanding myself)? Write about it here.

"To know what you truly value, you have to follow what makes you feel alive, what gives you enthusiasm, what raises goosebumps on your skin, what sends your imagination running wild."

—TOKO-PA TURNER

MY TOP VALUES

Your values act as a blueprint of what matters most to you in life. Rate each value in the following list with either a ++ (very important to me), + (kind of important to me), or—(not important to me) to discover your values. Sometimes, we highly rate the values that we know are expected of us. Instead, check in with yourself and confirm that what you identify as a value is coming from within. When you're done, reflect on the values that you rated highest.

_____ Acceptance/
self-acceptance

_____ Achievement

_____ Adventure

_____ Assertiveness

_____ Attractiveness

_____ Authenticity

_____ Autonomy

_____ Caring/self-care

_____ Challenge

_____ Compassion/
self-compassion

_____ Connection

_____ Contribution
and generosity

_____ Cooperation

_____ Courage

_____ Creativity

_____ Curiosity

_____ Dependability

_____ Ecology

_____ Encouragement

_____ Excitement

_____ Fairness and justice

_____ Fame

_____ Family

_____ Fitness

_____ Flexibility

_____ Forgiveness/
self-forgiveness

_____ Freedom and
independence

_____ Friendliness

_____ Fun and humor

_____ Gratitude

_____ Honesty

_____ Industry

_____ Inner peace

_____ Intelligence

_____ Intimacy

_____ Kindness

_____ Leisure

_____ Love

_____ Mindfulness

_____ Openness

_____ Order

_____ Persistence and
commitment

_____ Power

_____ Respect/self-respect

_____ Responsibility

_____ Safety and
protection

_____ Sensuality and
pleasure

_____ Sexuality

_____ Skillfulness

_____ Supportiveness

_____ Trust

REFLECT: Is there anywhere in your life that you've been acting out of fear and sacrificing or ignoring one or more of your values? (If you find it helpful, turn back to page 15 and browse through the "My Top Values" exercise.)

CENTER: Ask yourself, "What do my values suggest about how I want to live my life?" and "How would my life be different if I consistently let my values guide me to the people, actions, and situations that reflect what's important to me?" Write about it here.

ACT: Pick one of your most important personal values and commit to one small daily action you can take to live more in alignment with it starting today.

ALIGNING WITH MY SOUL

What things, people, or places do you feel deeply connected to that help you feel aligned with your soul? Fill in the following table and use it as a guide when you're at a loss for how to connect with your true self.

I feel most aligned with my soul when I am . . .

In These Places

Around These People

Around These Sorts of Things

Doing These Things

"The essence of a person is not the clothing she wears or the things he does . . . Your essence is not even your history, culture, race, or what you think and do. It is your soul."

—GARY ZUKAV

REFLECT: What makes you *you*? Jot down the things on which you tend to base your identity (e.g., your role as a mother, father, sister, or brother; your job; your past failures and successes; etc.).

CENTER: You aren't the job you have, the car you drive, your achievements, your past mistakes, or what you think yourself to be. That's what you see when you only know yourself as a personality. You—the real you— is who you are beneath and beyond all that. What words would you use to describe who you are and how you feel when you strip away the labels and roles of your personality?

ACT: Because the quality of your life consists of a series of small steps that you take every day, create a "mini-goal" or action step that you can regularly take to connect to your soul and remind yourself that you are not just a personality but a soul as well? (e.g., sitting in nature, meditating, journaling, looking at a photo of your younger self, etc.).

REFLECT: What does it mean to you to be spiritual? How does your sense of spirituality show up and help you in your daily life?

CENTER: One of the ways that spirituality can support you is by helping you move from identifying with your personality to identifying with your soul. How do you move through life when you identify with your personality? How do you move through life when you identify with your soul?

ACT: Your mind was going on and on about something recently. What was it? What does your soul want you to know about this thing, and what is one action you can take to honor your soul's message?

LIVING AUTHENTICALLY

Society's plan for me:

Whether it's been directly voiced to you or not, what does it seem that society's or your family's plan for your life looks like (e.g., getting married, staying married, having children, and/or buying a home, etc.)? Write, scribble, or draw it out.

My plan for me:

If you were to reveal your real self rather than contort yourself to what others want, what would you do and who would you be? Write, scribble, or draw it out.

Every day—including today—is a good day to see myself, know myself, love myself, and be myself.

REFLECT: Look back on the self-help or self-development work that you've done in the past (if you've done it). What were you hoping to improve in yourself?

CENTER: All sincere self-help and self-development roads lead back to the same place: You are enough, you are loved, and you matter just the way you are. How would your life be different if you knew you were enough—or, rather, more than enough—just as you are right now?

ACT: Take a deep breath and enjoy the realization that you are perfect just the way you are, that you're worthy of appreciating yourself with nothing to change, and that it's you in your "enoughness" that changes the world. Knowing you are enough, what is one action you can take in the direction of one of your goals?

REFLECT: Complete this sentence: *When I think about the future, something I am afraid of is . . .*

CENTER: Fear, like all emotions, isn't something to get rid of. The more we try to ignore or get rid of it, the louder it gets. When you consider that fear is simply letting you know that something doesn't feel safe, how would it be to turn toward rather than away from it?

ACT: Turn toward your fear and listen to what it's really here to tell you. If your fear could talk, what would it say? What is it hoping you'll understand? What does it need from you? And what is one step you can take to meet this need in the present so it occupies less mental and emotional space in your future?

CONNECTING TO MY INNER POWER

To connect to your inner power and see the things you do as choices rather than necessities, you can turn your "have-tos" into "choose-tos" and reflect on what desire of yours is driving that choice. For example, if you feel that you have to get up early for work, changing your have-to to choose-to would remind you that you are choosing to get up early for work because of what your job makes possible for you. Try it for a few days and notice how you feel.

I HAVE TO . . .	I CHOOSE TO . . .	BECAUSE I WANT TO . . .
get up early for work	get up early for work	contribute to the world in a meaningful way while contributing to my family's financial security

FURTHER REFLECTIONS

"Maybe the journey isn't so much about becoming anything. Maybe it's about unbecoming everything that isn't really you, so you can be who you were meant to be in the first place."

—PAULO COELHO

REFLECT: Imagine watching yourself from a distance. Describe what you see. How do you look, feel, and move? What are you doing? Are you living the kind of life you want to live?

CENTER: If you were living the kind of life you truly want to live, what feelings would you be feeling more often?

ACT: Pick one day this week and live this day to its fullest, as if it were your last. At the end of the day, take a few moments to reflect: What did you do differently on this day than you've done before? And what will you take away from this experience and bring with you into the rest of your life?

REFLECT: Who is a person around whom you've felt most loved and seen for who you truly are? What was/is so special about them?

CENTER: What we see in others is typically also a quality that we have within ourselves; otherwise we wouldn't be able to recognize it in another. How does it feel to know that you, too—to some degree—have the qualities that are so special and admirable within this other person?

ACT: Write down and elaborate on five things that are worthy of giving thanks for within yourself. As you do, invite yourself to really feel the feeling of appreciation behind the words.

When you're connected to and operating from your true self, you might notice that you feel different. Connect to your true self in whatever way feels best to you right now. (See the activity on connecting with your true self on page 17 for support if you'd like.) On the following "soul barometer," jot down how you feel when you're more connected to your soul and how you feel when you're less connected or totally disconnected from it. A few sample responses are provided to the left in gray.

CONNECTED TO MY SOUL

trusting of life

at ease

uneasy

overwhelmed

DISCONNECTED FROM MY SOUL

REFLECT: Does your life feel in or out of balance? If it feels out of balance, where in your relationships are you currently not honoring your energy, time, wants, and needs and sacrificing your internal peace and balance?

CENTER: It's easier to be who you want to be in life when you balance giving to others with giving to yourself. Can you notice the difference in who you are and who you can be when you approach your life from a place of balance rather than imbalance?

ACT: Rather than saying yes to someone else while saying no to yourself, sometimes it helps to say no to someone else so that you can first say yes to yourself. Where in your life can you say no right now to honor your energy, time, wants, and needs? Connect with your true self and take inspired action to say no where you need to.

BEAUTIFUL MOMENTS, PEOPLE, AND THINGS

Use the space to note down moments, people, and things you encounter throughout the day that you want to thank for finding their way into your life.

BEAUTIFUL MOMENTS	BEAUTIFUL PEOPLE	BEAUTIFUL THINGS

When my soul leads
and I follow,
everything
around me flows
with ease.

REFLECT: Ask yourself, "Are my beliefs about spirituality more similar to or different from the beliefs of my family?" and "How have my beliefs about spirituality been shaped by the people and ideas I grew up around?"

CENTER: Get curious for a moment. Is there a belief you adopted from how your parent(s) or primary caregivers(s) raised you that might be holding you back? What sorts of actions does this belief lead to in your life?

ACT: Reflecting on the belief you just wrote about, ask yourself, "What can I do to align my actions more with my individual beliefs rather than the beliefs I adopted from my family?" Take a small step in that direction today.

REFLECT: Complete this sentence and continue writing: *To me, being in alignment with my soul means . . .*

CENTER: Being in alignment with your soul is as much about what you don't do as it is about what you do. What are some behaviors that can interfere with your connection to your true self (e.g., keeping busy all the time, staying in unhealthy relationships, etc.)? How much easier would aligning with your true self be if these behaviors were less common?

ACT: If we engage in behaviors that deplete our alignment with our true self, sometimes it's because they offer some other (conscious or unconscious) benefit (e.g., helping ward off loneliness). Pick one of the behaviors that came to mind and ask yourself, "What benefit am I getting from this?" Is there an alternative way for you to get a similar benefit without sacrificing your ability to live in alignment with your true self?

BECOMING AWARE OF HOW I DISCONNECT FROM MYSELF

Habits that you knowingly or unknowingly have can hinder your alignment with your soul. Which of these habits are ways that you abandon your dedication to your true self? Add any others that you are aware of that are not mentioned here.

When you're done, look over your checklist with kind and compassionate awareness, knowing that we develop habits of disconnecting from ourselves because we may not know another way (i.e., we weren't taught early on that our needs and feelings are important).

☐ Comparing myself to others

☐ Distracting myself by filling every moment of my day

☐ Ignoring my heart's desires

☐ Overexplaining myself

☐ Trying to be perfect

☐ Giving a lot of love "out there" and not enough "in here"

☐ Staying busy so I don't have to think

☐ Trying to control the people and events in my life

☐ ....

☐ ....

☐ Avoiding responsibility for my mistakes

☐ Overfocusing on my performance

☐ Resisting my unpleasant feelings

☐ Not giving my feelings a voice

☐ Seeking validation from other people

☐ Disguising my authentic self to be liked

☐ Not reinforcing my boundaries

☐ Focusing on other people's needs and ignoring my own

☐ ....

☐ ....

REFLECT: Escaping being with yourself in the present moment can take the form of keeping yourself stimulated with things like work or distracted with TV or social media. What are some ways that you escape being with yourself in the present moment?

CENTER: How do you think it might affect your relationships and your life if you were to no longer try to escape the present moment and the emotions that come along with it? How would your life change by allowing yourself time and space to be with yourself and your emotions?

ACT: Start where you are. What are you feeling right now? Where in your body are you feeling it? Turn inward and describe the emotion and how it shows up in your body (e.g., tension in the shoulders, tightness in the chest, vibrating feeling or pressure in the head, etc.). Let yourself observe and describe whatever you feel, and notice any urge or desire that you may have to move toward a distraction, too.

REFLECT: Gather some curiosity and ask yourself, "Am I simply going through the motions of my life, or am I really living it?" What makes you say that?

CENTER: The ability to engage in your life with slow, deliberate, and intentional pursuits is an antidote to the automatic, habitual ways of living that many are used to. How might bringing more consciousness to your actions change the way you think, feel, and live?

ACT: To move consciously and intentionally about your life, it helps to create an intention for the various parts of your day. For each segment of your day, write a corresponding intention of how you want to show up during that time frame (e.g., authentic, compassionate, flexible, grateful, present, etc.). Add additional segments that suit your particular schedule and life.

Before I log on to social media . . .

Intention:

Before I log on/walk in to work for the day . . .

Intention:

When someone walks into the room . . .

Intention:

REFLECT: How do you tend to respond to people amid conflict, anger, or frustration?

CENTER: Knowing that you have a choice in how you respond to the situations of your life, envision yourself responding more constructively in moments of conflict rather than reacting in a habitual, knee-jerk way. How would your life be different if you could respond with more empathy and respect in these moments?

ACT: To help you respond in the way you want to rather than the way you're used to, anchor a new response to the first thing you notice in conflict. For example, if the first thing you're aware of amid conflict is that you grow angry and defensive, you might anchor this new habit: "When I notice myself getting into a defensive posture, I will say that I need some time to myself before I can continue on with the conversation."

Your turn: *After I* ....,

I will ....

FURTHER REFLECTIONS

When I remember
and align with
who I truly am,
the only way
life can be
is beautiful.

REFLECT: When you look back on your life, do you think that people meet by happenstance or that there's a reason for their meeting? Are there any examples in your own life?

CENTER: If you adopt the notion that there may very well be a reason for meeting every person you meet, how would that affect your sense of meaning in life?

ACT: Try on the idea that every person you meet offers either a lesson or a blessing. Reflect on the last three people that have come into your life and ask yourself: "Lesson or blessing?" Write about what each offered you by coming into your life when and how they did.

REFLECT: Do you tend to focus more on what you can *get from* life or on what you can *give to* life? Do you find yourself intending for the betterment of *your own* life or for the betterment of *all* life?

CENTER: When you give to the people around you, how does it affect your sense of meaning? Purpose? Joy? Does giving to others make you feel more or less connected to your true self?

ACT: What is one new way that you can give to your neighbors, friends, or community? Write about how you intend to give back within the next week and beyond, and remember, giving to others doesn't need to be extravagant; simple can be quite impactful, too. Then reflect on this question: "How does the betterment of all life impact my own?"

CONNECTING TO MYSELF

Spend five minutes in silence and stillness to connect to your heart and soul. When you're done, go on to read the sentence and write, sketch, or draw whatever comes to mind.

What I really want in life right now is . . .

FURTHER REFLECTIONS

REFLECT: Whom have you judged or criticized lately? As you think about the person and what judgments you had of them, take note of how you feel. Does your heart feel open or closed? Do you feel lighter or heavier? Happier or not?

CENTER: Judging others is a normal human experience. At the same time, making fewer judgments can work wonders for your relationships and emotional well-being. How do you think turning your assumptions and judgments (e.g., "You are wrong or not okay") into curiosities (e.g., "What is it like to be you?") would make you feel?

ACT: Take the assumptions and judgments you just wrote about and turn them into curiosities. The easiest way to do that is to turn whatever you might be thinking into a question by saying to yourself, "I wonder why they did/said that" or "I've never been in that situation before. What might it be like?"

This set of prompts refers to relationship challenges and may be triggering for some readers, so please read with discretion. If you are experiencing sexual, emotional, and/or physical abuse in a relationship, know you are not alone and be sure to use discernment and please seek help.

REFLECT: Is there someone in your life who is currently at the root of your sadness, anger, frustration, or stress? What did they do, and why are they to blame?

CENTER: With each negative experience, we can point the finger at someone else, or we can turn inward and consider that every experience is also here to help us learn about or heal something within. How might choosing to learn and grow from a hurtful situation affect your ability to resolve and move on from it?

ACT: If the experiences and people who you consider tormentors can also be your mentors or teachers, what might this person or adversity be here to teach you? For example, is this situation bringing up some hurt or insecurity of yours that's been lying deep below the surface and giving you an opportunity to listen to, understand, and bring love to it? Or is this situation urging you to learn to create boundaries or leave situations or relationships that are not good for you?

REFLECT: Complete this sentence and continue writing: *My deepest wish for the world is . . .*

CENTER: We change the world primarily by changing ourselves. What kind of change do you think is possible in the world when a single person transforms something within themselves?

ACT: Choose a quality or part of yourself that, if healed or transformed, would bring you closer to being the way you want the world to be. Knowing that transformation happens when we embrace and love what we find within ourselves, open your heart and offer this part of you some words and/or gestures of tenderness and kindness. Reflect on the experience here.

FURTHER REFLECTIONS

REFLECT: Have you ever felt bad about yourself because of your job, weight, income, wardrobe, zip code, dating or marital status, educational level, productivity level, or something else? When?

CENTER: You are and always have been worthy and valuable simply because you exist. Your worth has never been dependent on any external factors like what you say, do, weigh, or wear. How would you treat yourself differently if you knew, without a doubt, that this was true?

ACT: Put on your "soul glasses." These are the imaginary glasses that let you see beyond appearances and help you recognize the soul essence in everyone, including yourself. Fill in each blank on the following page with something that you've hung your self-worth on in the past. Say the statements aloud to yourself today and use them as affirmations to repeat to yourself anytime you need. The first line is provided as an example.

My job title may change, but my worth will not.

_____ may change, but my worth will not.

_____ may change, but my worth will not.

_____ may change, but my worth will not.

_____ may change, but my worth will not.

_____ may change, but my worth will not.

_____ may change, but my worth will not.

_____ may change, but my worth will not.

_____ may change, but my worth will not.

_____ may change, but my worth will not.

_____ may change, but my worth will not.

THE "BUTS" THAT LIMIT MY DREAMS

Without self-judgment or shame, bring to mind the "buts" that are stopping you from getting closer to your dreams.

For each dream you wrote, sketched, or drew on page 50 for the "Connecting to Myself" exercise), list at least one "but" (e.g., "but I don't know how," "but I'm just not _____ enough"). Then think about and write down what you can begin to do today to courageously address each of these "buts" (e.g., "reach out for the support I need," "reconnect to my true essence," "learn something new," etc.).

MY DREAM	BUT . . .	HOW I WILL BEGIN TO ADDRESS THIS "BUT"

THE PARTS OF MY PERSONALITY

Your personality is made of many distinct parts with different needs—some that are based in your true nature of love and others that are based in fear. It's okay; we all have both. What parts make up your personality? Circle the love-driven parts of yourself, underline the fear-driven parts of yourself. When you're done, put on your "soul glasses," and look over the page with kindness and understanding.

Inner critic	Angry	Worrier	Multitasker	Overeater	Spontaneous
Appearance-focused	Impulsive	Blamer	Creative	Hurt	Overthinker
Skeptic	Honest	Jealous	Friendly	Upset	Calm
Distrustful	Supportive	Lonely	Angry	Perfectionist	Compassionate
Sensitive	Scared	Planner	Intellectualizer	Trusting	Confident
Impatient	Courageous	Need to be right	Pessimist	Ultra-independent	People-pleaser
Overachiever	Discerning	Competitive	Lighthearted	Intuitive	Procrastinator

Inner critic	Angry	Worrier	Multitasker	Overeater	Spontaneous
Selfish	Rebel	Gentle	Nurturer	Resentful	Workaholic
Kind	Exhausted	Assertive	Hopeless	Inner cheerleader	Patient
Joyful	Genuine	Brave	Controlling	Ashamed	Consistent
Playful	Present	Open-minded	Insecure	Defensive	Judgmental
Fearful	Confused	Health-conscious			

BRINGING UNDERSTANDING TO FEAR-DRIVEN PARTS OF MY PERSONALITY

Pick one fear-driven part of your personality from the exercise on page 102 and instead of turning away from it, open your heart to it. Maintaining the perspective of your true self and the understanding that this part of you arose as a coping strategy to protect you based on your past, write it a short message. Offer it understanding for why it exists and express gratitude, forgiveness, or whatever feels right to you. It's not possible to change anything about yourself or about life without befriending and embracing it first.

REFLECT: Do you feel that you often have control over what you say or do? Or does it feel like sometimes your words and actions are choosing you?

CENTER: Consciously choosing your actions may seem difficult if you're not willing to understand and be with the fear-driven parts of you that really want to shape them. How do you think it might help you to be curious and understanding to the fear-driven parts of you, rather than judging and suppressing them?

ACT: Recall a recent decision you made that didn't lead to an outcome you liked. Ask yourself, "Why did I make that decision?" After answering, again ask, "Why?" Then ask "Why?" five more times or as many times as you need to get to the core reason behind your decision. When you're done, offer understanding and love to whatever remains (e.g., sadness, anger, loneliness, concern, etc.).

REFLECT: Whether in your relationships, your work, or your community, think back to a time when your actions led to an outcome that you didn't like. What happened?

CENTER: Anytime you act, it's from a place of fear, worry, and self-protection or from a place of love, vulnerability, and connection. In the situation you thought of, were you mostly acting from fear-driven or love-driven parts of you? How do you think that impacted the outcome?

ACT: Think of a situation in your life where the fear- and love-driven parts of you are both vying to be expressed and acted upon. Invite yourself to see what your fear-driven parts really want for you in this situation (e.g., safety, understanding, protection, care, etc.). How can you offer your fear-driven parts what they need most? Take some time to offer what's needed through a word, gesture, or action of some sort. Then reflect on how addressing the deeper needs of fear-driven parts of you might help you act less from self-protection and more from love and connection in the future.

REFLECT: Think back to the last big decision you made. Pause to think: Who made that decision? Was it a deeper aspect of you (i.e., your soul)? Or was it a part of your personality that was feeling hurt, afraid, or insecure? How did this decision turn out?

CENTER: When your personality makes decisions *together* with your soul, you can rest assured that your decisions are supporting and aligning with your inner wisdom. When you think about your life, what kind of mental, emotional, and spiritual space do you want to be in when making decisions?

ACT: What is one decision that you need to make right now? Write about the preferences that the hurt, insecure, or fear-driven parts of your personality have for this situation. Next, write about the wisdom and preference your soul has for this situation. What would a soul-based decision be in this situation? If you don't feel able to make a soul-based decision, remember that it is always okay to wait before deciding altogether.

REFLECT: Where in your life are you trying to protect another person, yourself, or both by not sharing your truth (e.g., protecting them from feeling rejected or protecting yourself from feeling rejected by their potential response)?

CENTER: Every time we share what's meaningfully true for us—whether we're expressing love, hurt, or desire—we make it known that our own truth and the truth of others is important. Who do you think you'd be if you were to stop withholding your truth and instead chose to own it?

ACT: Identify a stable and meaningful truth of yours (e.g., how important it is for you to give and receive kindness, even when opinions clash), not just a temporary truth that came up during a fleeting period of irritation or dissatisfaction (e.g., that you find your friend to be selfish). Jot down what you want to express and how you plan to say it with care and grace. When you feel ready, bring your courageous heart along, and take ownership of what you're thinking and how you're feeling by voicing your truth.

TUNING IN TO THE VOICE OF MY SOUL

Emotions are much more a source of information than they are a source of identity. For example, sadness might be a message from your soul that there is something unresolved in your heart seeking your attention, and anxiety might be letting you know that your mind and heart are in disagreement on something. What message are your emotions sending you? To find out, turn inward and fill in the chart anytime you feel an unpleasant emotion.

EMOTION I'M FEELING	MESSAGE IT IS SENDING ME

"The resting place of the mind is the heart . . . The only place the mind will ever find peace is inside the silence of the heart. That's where you need to go."

—ELIZABETH GILBERT

REFLECT: Do you remember the last time someone accepted you fully? What did they say or do that made you feel fully loved for who you are?

CENTER: The greatest gift you can give anyone is to love and accept them exactly as they are. How did it feel to receive this gift of love and full acceptance? How did it affect your life? And how do you think offering the same gift to others might impact their lives?

ACT: Think of one person you care about who could benefit from knowing they are loved as they are. How can you offer them this gift (e.g., through a gesture, word, action, or even silence perhaps)?

REFLECT: Ask yourself, "Whom have I hurt in the past that I feel guilty, ashamed, or remorseful about hurting?" Describe what happened and how you knew that the other person was hurt.

CENTER: When you can acknowledge your humanness and forgive yourself, you get closer to your true nature. How has carrying guilt, shame, or remorse all this time affected you? Who would you be without it?

ACT: Forgiving yourself doesn't mean you forget. It means you free yourself of the burden of the experience and stop wishing that it would've been different. Write a short message of kindness to the version of you who didn't know what you know now and was able to hurt someone in the way they did. Show yourself understanding and compassion and, only if it feels right (don't rush into it), offer yourself forgiveness.

FURTHER REFLECTIONS

A CONVERSATION WITH MY FUTURE SELF

Create a dialogue between you and your future self who is 10 or 20 years older and wiser. Ask what they suggest you spend your time and energy on. Listen for and write down an answer. Then ask any questions to which you're "dying" to know the answer, and respond how you imagine your future self would. If you need a boost to connect with your heart, try writing with your nondominant hand when writing as your future self. Feel free to continue on the "further reflections" pages of this book if you'd like.

Me:

My Future Self:

Me:

My Future Self:

Me:

My Future Self:

Me:

My Future Self:

Today, someone's
day will
be better
because of me.

REFLECT: Think of a problem you're having right now. What about this situation is difficult, burdensome, or complicated?

CENTER: Sometimes, solutions to your problems may appear hidden, unavailable, or completely nonexistent when you ruminate and think rationally about the details. If you were to stop thinking about this problem and instead connected to and trusted the wisdom of your soul, what do you think might happen?

ACT: Connect to your soul in whatever way feels best to you right now (feel free to turn to page 50 for ideas). Take a moment to see this situation from the point of view of your true self and to see the true self of anyone else involved. From that perspective, what seems to be a good solution? Whatever the small first step is that you can take in that direction, take it.

REFLECT: To whom or where do you typically go for guidance? A good friend? Family member? Google? Why?

CENTER: If you have friends or family to turn to for guidance in life, you are fortunate. But no matter who you are, you also have an inherent wisdom that comes from a place deeper than your fears, anxiety, intellect, or even family and friends. Who would you be if you tapped into and trusted your inner knowing without needing someone else to approve or validate it?

ACT: Turn inward and think of something you want guidance on. Then bring to mind various directions that you can take in the situation. Notice how your body responds to each one. Does it expand and feel more alive, symbolizing a positive or "yes" response? Or does it contract and get stiffer, symbolizing more of a negative or "no" response? Once you have a sense of the direction you want to head in, choose one small way to honor this insight from your soul today. Write about your experience of turning inward for guidance here.

CREATING A MEANINGFUL ROUTINE

Write out your weekly routine, look it over, and ask yourself: "Is there meaning in my routine?" If the components of your routine aren't bringing any meaning or enough meaning to your life, what can you change about them? The more you align your thoughts and actions with the desires of your soul, the more meaning you will feel day to day.

	MORNING	AFTERNOON	EVENING
Monday			
Tuesday			
Wednesday			
Thursday			
Friday			
Saturday			
Sunday			

"The point of life is not to get anywhere-it is to notice that you are, and have always been, already there."

—NEALE DONALD WALSCH

REFLECT: How often do you engage in mindless activities like endlessly watching television, snacking, or scrolling through social media?

CENTER: What would your life be like if you were able to swap these stand-in behaviors (i.e., behaviors that are meant to fill the emptiness left by a lack of joy or meaning) for soul-nourishing ones?

ACT: The next time you catch yourself tempted to fill the emptiness of your heart, instead of jumping into the activity, let yourself be with yourself. Notice your thoughts and emotions, and feel any physical sensations present in your body. Write about the experience of being with yourself here.

REFLECT: Do you ever make assumptions and jump to conclusions about yourself based on your thoughts? Consider, for example, what the thoughts and feelings you're having at this moment tell you about you.

CENTER: You are not your thoughts and feelings. You're the one who thinks and feels them. Each thought and feeling is simply a friend visiting you with a message, and you don't have to be ashamed, embarrassed, or consumed by it. How do you think being able to notice—rather than identify with—your thoughts and feelings can help you relax into your true self?

ACT: Knowing that each thought and feeling is a friend passing by to share something with you, it doesn't make sense to deny, refuse, or silence your thoughts and feelings. Instead, you can slow down to acknowledge, feel, and listen to them with curiosity. Ask yourself: "What am I feeling?" and "What do I need most in this moment?"

REFLECT: As you move through life, do you notice an urge to hurry? If so, when and how does it show up for you?

CENTER: We often rush because we're afraid of missing life's moments (e.g., not accomplishing everything we want to). Yet it's when we slow down that we miss less of life because we can truly be present in each moment. How might it affect your day to consciously slow down as you move between people, places, and activities?

ACT: As you go from place to place today, deliberately let yourself just be in each new environment. For up to a minute, as you enter each new setting, look inward and notice how your mind and body feel. At the end of the day, reflect on and write about the experience of pausing intentionally in this way.

FURTHER REFLECTIONS

Slowly and joyfully is the way. Slowly and joyfully is *my way.*

CHOOSING WHAT I BELIEVE

Children often don't get to decide what to believe; they unconsciously adopt the belief systems of the people around them. But getting older often means understanding that we have that choice. Fill out the following chart to get a glimpse into what you were taught to believe and what you're choosing to believe today. Then consider how you can reinforce the latter while unlearning the former throughout your life. An example is provided in the first row.

	WHAT DID MY PAST EXPERIENCES LEAD ME TO BELIEVE ABOUT THIS?	WHAT ARE MY PERSONAL BELIEFS ABOUT THIS THAT I'D LIKE TO REINFORCE THROUGHOUT THE REST OF MY LIFE?	HOW CAN I UNLEARN MY PAST BELIEF AND/OR REINFORCE THE BELIEF THAT I AM BUILDING?
Love	Love can be tumultuous and unpredictable.	Love can be safe and comforting with the right people.	Open my heart, just a little bit, to people who I consider to be capable of emotionally healthy love.
Love			
Sex			
Money			

	WHAT DID MY PAST EXPERIENCES LEAD ME TO BELIEVE ABOUT THIS?	WHAT ARE MY PERSONAL BELIEFS ABOUT THIS THAT I'D LIKE TO REINFORCE THROUGHOUT THE REST OF MY LIFE?	HOW CAN I UNLEARN MY PAST BELIEF AND/OR REINFORCE THE BELIEF THAT I AM BUILDING?
Problems			
Conflict			
Gender Roles			
Good/Bad Behavior			
Good/Bad People			
The Universe/God/ Spirituality			
Myself			

FURTHER REFLECTIONS

"... *life is a gift and our only purpose is to be who we are. We all make it so complicated, and try to find our purpose. I learned that all I have to do is be as me as I can be.*"

—ANITA MOORJANI

REFLECT: Do you have or have you ever had a spiritual practice—something that helps you bring love and joy into your heart and connects you to your soul? If so, what was/is it, and how did/does it support you?

CENTER: Having a spiritual practice can help you connect to your soul intentionally, authentically, and consistently. What is one spiritual practice that aligns with your beliefs (e.g., sitting in silence for a few minutes, lighting a candle and saying a prayer, reading a page from a spiritual book, etc.)? What about it makes or would make it a meaningful practice for you?

ACT: Take the spiritual practice you thought of and turn it into a sacred daily ritual to create a bridge between your inner world and your outer world. If you already have a sacred ritual, take a moment to feel into whether you can fine-tune any of its elements (e.g., add a candle, replace a photo, etc.) to best suit what you need at this phase of your life.

REFLECT: Think about the last thing you did (e.g., talking to someone at the gro-cery store, feeding your pet, etc.). What do you think the effects of this action were on the people around you and on the world? How would the world be if you hadn't done that?

CENTER: We are, in every moment, affecting and affected by everything going on around us. Everything that happens is a reaction to something that's happened before it. How does it feel to know that what you do affects the world and that you are inher-ently powerful through the choices you make and actions you take?

ACT: Let your intention today be to let everything you do be a cause of greater joy and understanding in the world. Knowing that there is no loving action that is too small to positively shape the world, what are two small actions you can take to honor this intention? Go out and do them.

REFLECT: Day to day, is your focus more on doing things right or on doing the right things? How so?

CENTER: People often spend their lives focused on doing things right, whether or not those things really nourish them rather than doing the right things (i.e., those that bring meaning and satisfaction to their lives). How might shifting your focus from doing things right to doing the right things help you live a more authentic and purposeful life?

ACT: Go through your calendar for the month, and find something you habitually do that doesn't bring you meaning and satisfaction. What's the first step you can take to remove this from your daily life and replace it with something more fulfilling and right for you? If you think there might be a deeper fear underlying this thing you do (e.g., not getting validation), feel free to revisit page 102.

FURTHER REFLECTIONS

THOUGHTS ON THE STREAM

Imagine taking every thought you're having right now (no matter if it's painful, pleasurable, or somewhere in between) and placing each one on a leaf floating down a river. If it helps you, concretize your thoughts by drawing 10 leaves in the blank space that follows, jotting a thought down on each one and then imagining the thoughts pass without rushing them along. Be present with them as they pass, and when you flip the page, visualize that they've naturally drifted in and out of the river of your mind.

I trust the ways in
which my soul
is moving me
to evolve.

REFLECT: What does spirituality mean to you? And what does it mean about you? Would you say that you are a spiritual being having a human experience or a human being having a spiritual experience?

CENTER: From the perspective of your soul and true nature, you are a spiritual being having a human experience. And if that's the case, then there is more to your life than what you see, feel, smell, taste, and hear, right? In what ways can this perspective help you?

ACT: Choose a day and consciously walk through it as a spiritual being having a human experience. Notice what your human self allows you to know with your five senses and what your spiritual self allows you to know and be that isn't possible simply with your five senses. At the end of the day, write about the ways in which your spiritual nature helped you on this day.

REFLECT: Do you focus most on the big moments of your life or on the little day-to-day events? Why?

CENTER: When you consciously pay attention to the little moments of your life, it's much easier to find things to appreciate. How do you think life would be different if you let the little moments that make up much of your life (like the feeling of the sunshine, a warm cup of coffee, or a moment of laughter) really touch your heart and soul?

ACT: Take five minutes to look back on your day. What was good about it? Feel (and write, if you prefer) genuine appreciation for all the good that this day brought.

UNDERSTANDING DISCREPANCIES BETWEEN MY BEHAVIORS AND VALUES

What are your top five values? Reference page 15 and write them down in the left-hand column of the following table. Next, using ++ (very consistent), + (kind of consistent), or − (inconsistently), evaluate how consistent your day-to-day actions over the past year have been with each value. For each instance of inconsistent behavior you remember, take a few moments to think about why you may have behaved in that way, focusing on the fears or beliefs of yours that might have been at play and doing so with curiosity and without judgment. An example is provided in the first row.

MY VALUE	HOW CONSISTENT?	EXAMPLES OF INCONSISTENCY	FEARS OR BELIEFS AT PLAY
Authenticity	+	When Gail asked about the interview, I lied and said it went well.	I didn't want to be seen as unintelligent, incapable, or inflexible.

This exercise was inspired by Keith Merron, EdD, author of Inner Freedom: Authentically Living the Life You Were Truly Meant to Live *by Integral Publishers.*

FURTHER REFLECTIONS

"We carry inside us the wonders we seek outside us."

—RUMI

REFLECT: Complete the sentence: *Right now, I am not totally at peace with*

....*, and I am trying to rectify it by*

....

CENTER: It's not changing other people or situations that brings you the peace you seek, but rather changing yourself and your own thinking. How do you think the outside world might respond to you shifting on the inside?

ACT: Relax your shoulders, loosen any tension in your forehead, and unclench your jaw. Simply direct your attention inward, and for two to three minutes, become aware of how your personality is making sense of the situation. For another two to three minutes, let yourself see the situation through the eyes of your true self. What does your true self know and want you to know about this situation?

REFLECT: Do you have a passion, story, interest, talent, or idea that you haven't yet expressed in your life?

CENTER: When you listen to and trust your inner voice, the desires of your soul become hard to ignore. If you were to regularly listen to and act on the truth of your intuitive inner voice, would your life be any different than it is now? How?

ACT: To say yes to the passion, story, interest, talent, or idea that you've yet to express, is there something that you first need to say no to? How can you start to make this shift so that you can express your soul's truth more and more?

I welcome whatever experience life brings me, whether pain or joy. I let there be room for it all.

REFLECT: Think back to the last time you gave someone a gift. Whether it was a gift of your time, presence, or talent or a material thing, how did it feel to give?

CENTER: What do you think it is about helping others that makes it a gift not just for them but also for you?

ACT: Who are three people to whom you'd like to give some sort of gift? What is one thing you can do right now—no matter how small—that improves life for each of these people? Go ahead and give them your gift. As you do, let yourself feel the love you have for them. Notice how it feels in your body, mind, and heart to give.

WHAT IS ALIVE IN ME RIGHT NOW?

Ask yourself: "What is alive in me right now?" Draw, write, or sketch out any thoughts, emotions, and physical sensations that are part of your inner world right now. Use up as much of the page as you want. When you feel that you've finished, look over the page with acceptance and without judgment.

When I accept and
love myself, the
whole world
feels it.

REFLECT: Every day consists of 1,440 minutes. How many of those minutes do you spend making a positive impact on the world around you? In what ways?

CENTER: You never really know the impact that your kindness has on someone's life. Maybe the way you listened was just what someone needed, or perhaps your smile instantaneously turned someone's entire day around. How do you feel knowing that your kindness has a true impact on those around you, often far beyond what you see?

ACT: If we want to be regularly kind, it helps to make kindness an intentional and conscious activity. Write a list of ways that you can be kind or help someone right now in your life (e.g., giving something you no longer need, leaving a note of thanks, extending an invitation, offering a hug, etc.). Do one thing on the list every day for the next seven days. Then reflect on how you feel.

REFLECT: Have you ever considered that stress and worry don't come from what's going on in your life but from your thoughts about what's going on in your life? If so, what prompted you to consider it?

CENTER: You don't get to choose what you think and how you feel. You do, however, get to choose how you relate to what you think and how you feel. When you allow your thoughts and feelings to exist, knowing that they are temporary, you will be less controlled by them. If you were less controlled by your unpleasant thoughts and feelings, how would your life be different?

ACT: Sit in a comfortable seat, set a timer for five minutes, and observe your thoughts, feelings, and physical sensations with openness and compassion rather than criticism. Welcome any thoughts or feelings, whether pleasant or unpleasant, as you would a visitor in your home. When the five minutes are up, write about the experience in the space below.

FURTHER REFLECTIONS

"Your problem is how you are going to spend this one odd and precious life you have been issued. Whether you're going to spend it trying to look good and creating the illusion that you have power over people and circumstances, or whether you are going to taste it, enjoy it and find out the truth about who you are."

—ANNE LAMOTT

REFLECT: Think back to the last time you felt off. Were you doing something that was depleting your physical, emotional, and spiritual energy or not doing something to maintain it?

CENTER: If you're not feeling your best, chances are you've been neglecting your physical, emotional, and spiritual self. Who are you when your various physical, emotional, and spiritual needs *aren't* being met? Who are you when they *are*?

ACT: Place one hand on your heart and the other on your belly. Breathe in and out deeply. Repeat twice more. Then ask yourself, "What needs of mine have been sneaking under the radar? What needs of mine can I make time to honor today?" Then do it. Prioritize your needs and replenish your physical, emotional, and spiritual self.

REFLECT: Pick a relationship in your life that could use some improvement. What do you wish would be better about it?

CENTER: What is one quality or feeling that lets you know you're connected to and operating from your emotion? (Feel free to turn back to the exercise on page 69 for ideas.) Bring this soul quality to yourself through a meaningful action, gesture, or word. For example, if the quality is understanding, maybe you place your hand on your heart and tell yourself, "I understand how you feel; no wonder you're feeling that way."

ACT: Now apply the soul quality you picked to the relationship you chose, either verbally or through a meaningful action or gesture. Often, it's easier to extend a quality to others once we've offered it first to ourselves. How does bringing this soul quality into your relationship impact the other person? How does it impact you? How does it impact the relationship between you?

REFLECT: How do you feel about the world around you? Do you find it to be a good or bad place? Fair or unfair? Full of misery or full of hope?

CENTER: Think about a time when you were deeply in love with the world and felt entirely at peace within yourself. How do you think your life would be if you were able to access this state of being more readily?

ACT: The better you feel about yourself, the better you feel about the world. The more you love yourself, the more you align with the energy of love and can love the world. Write a note of loving appreciation to yourself by filling in this statement 10 times: *Thank you for being . . .* When you're done writing, read the note aloud to yourself.

REFLECT: In what ways do you reject the life you've created for yourself (e.g., dreaming of a different partner, constantly imagining a better job or a different home, etc.)?

CENTER: The grass often seems greener on the other side, but it isn't always actually greener. What if you could appreciate and enjoy the life you have now without rejecting it? How do you think that would feel?

ACT: Invite yourself to embrace your current life and love it despite its shortcomings. Ask yourself, "In what ways do I already love my life?" Write down five things that come to mind. It's by embracing your life as it is that you allow it to become what it's meant to be.

The three steps
to my happy life:
  1) lean into my soul,
  2) honor its
      whispers, and
  3) linger in
      gratitude.

REFLECT: If people create themselves through the choices they make every day, what kind of person are you creating? Is the person you're creating the person you want to be?

CENTER: Your true self walks hand in hand with your heart and makes choices from a centered, loving, and trusting place. How does it feel to know that when aligned with your true self, your choices will come from a place of love, calm, and self-trust instead of fear and self-doubt?

ACT: Tap into your true self. If your true self and not your conditioned self or personality were choosing how you spend your time this week, what would you do more of (e.g., take a risk or leap of faith, connect with the people around you)? What might you do less of (e.g., procrastinate on a goal you're pursuing, talk yourself out of a dream you have, make a decision purely out of pressure to conform, etc.)? Let the hours of your day more closely match the desires of your true self this week. At the end of the week, reflect on and write about the experience.

REFLECT: What do you see when you look in the mirror, and what do you say if you're asked to describe yourself? Do you think the way you see yourself impacts how capable you are of living from your soul's intentions and desires?

CENTER: How do you think your life would be different if you consistently saw your-self the way the Universe/God/Spirit/your Higher Self sees you?

ACT: Close your eyes and let the fears, concerns, and doubts of your personality fall away. Imagine seeing yourself from the perspective of the Universe/God/Spirit/your personal source of spirituality. Open your eyes and draw or write out what you see. From this space, choose a desire of yours and act on it today.

THE PAGE OF REASONS

This is the page of reasons. In the circle, write: *The reason I'm alive is...* Around it, write all the reasons that come to mind as to why you, exactly as you are, exist.

FURTHER REFLECTIONS

"Within you there is a stillness and a sanctuary to which you can retreat at any time and be yourself."

—HERMANN HESSE

REFLECT: Were you taught to love all parts of you or only the perfect and ideal ones? How often have you criticized and blamed yourself for being flawed, imperfect, and human?

CENTER: Becoming who you want to be is less about fixing yourself and more about accepting all of yourself. Imagine for a moment holding—with appreciation and compassion—not just the perfect and socially favorable parts of you but also those that are fearful, quirky, or seen as "negative." How does it feel?

ACT: Close the gap between who you are and who you want to be by taking the shame out of who you are. Create your own affirmation by filling in the blanks with aspects of yourself that you've deemed "negative." Repeat it to yourself as often as you want or need.

I love myself even though I can be a bit .... *and*

.... *sometimes.*

REFLECT: What is something you've received from those who came before you—whether your parents or grandparents, a member of your community, or an ancestor—that has made your life easier in some way?

CENTER: How do you think the meaningful messages, legacies, or experiences that are passed down impact us and our lives? Imagine what the world would be like if more people opened their hearts and lovingly gave to the people around them.

ACT: What is something you can give in return for all that you've received in life so far? Tune in to your heart and think of one action you can take this week to contribute to the love in the world. When you're done, reflect on and write about it in the space below.

REFLECT: How do you usually respond to life's ebbs and flows? Do you relax into whatever's happening, whether it's pleasure, pain, or somewhere in between? Or do you tend to pull joy and love toward you and push sadness, fear, frustration, and overwhelm away?

CENTER: Happiness in life doesn't come from everything going your way but rather from relaxing into life's moments, whether they're pleasurable or painful. What if today you could stop trying to curate a life that's only filled with pleasure and instead relaxed into its flow? How might that feel?

ACT: Practice saying yes to everything that arises in your life. Write down a list of things currently occupying your mental and emotional energy. Look over the list, and as you pause with each item, say a soft and wholehearted yes to it. Then move on to the next.

I forgive myself for every time I chose external validation and approval over authenticity.

REFLECT: Who has made a meaningful impact on your life? Who has offered you kindness, lifted you up, or made your life easier when you needed it most? Describe what they did and how it affected you.

CENTER: Often, people get so busy with their own lives that they forget to extend kindness and compassion to others. Step into the shoes of the person who was kind to you or made your life easier. How did extending this kindness to you affect them?

ACT: Who can you lift up as you've been lifted up? How can you make someone else's life easier? This week, add the question "What can I do for *you*?" to your day-to-day conversations and see what arises. How did it feel to shift focus from you to the people around you? How do you think they felt being the recipients of your kind thoughts and perhaps actions, too?

FURTHER REFLECTIONS

"There is nothing more important to true growth than realizing that you are not the voice of the mind—you are the one who hears it . . ."

—MICHAEL A. SINGER

REFLECT: Have you ever taken the good things in life for granted? A relationship with a partner or friend? A conversation with a neighbor? A smile from a stranger? Think of some things that you've personally taken for granted.

CENTER: It's a normal human experience to take things for granted, yet when you do, it's almost like giving away the things you've been granted. Ask yourself this: "If my life dramatically changed next week, what would I miss most? Why?"

ACT: Transform your appreciation into action. Based on what you wrote, is there someone to whom you need to say "I appreciate you" or "I love you"? Do it and notice how you feel.

REFLECT: Is there any area of your life where you "talk the talk" more than you "walk the walk" when it comes to your values? Is there anywhere that you're choosing what's easy over what's right? If so, where? How?

CENTER: How might life be if you were to live in integrity more by living by your values rather than simply being distracted by things that don't matter or doing things just because they're convenient or help you fit in with the rest of the world?

ACT: To get back into integrity, it helps to pause and consider your truth. Start by filling in the blank with a value that's important to you when it comes to this area of your life where you seem to be "talking the talk" more than "walking the walk": *What's true and important for* me *in this area of my life is* _____. Then consider one step you can take to honor this inner truth and realign with your true self. (Feel free to reference page 15 for the exercise on identifying your values if you'd like.)

REFLECT: There is something that nobody knows about you because you've done a really good job at hiding it. Why haven't you shared it with anyone? What are you afraid people would think and feel about you if they knew?

CENTER: The greatest reward of the path of authenticity is being truly seen and loved for who you are. If you knew that true freedom awaited you on the other side of letting yourself be fully seen and known (versus just letting certain parts of you be seen), would you do it?

ACT: Tap into the courageous part of you that wants you to be seen and known as you are. Choose someone you trust and who you know will respond to your transparency with love and acceptance. Reveal your hidden truth to them and notice how you feel in the days and weeks that follow.

REFLECTING ON MY SPIRITUAL JOURNEY

Like a forest path that veers in many directions along streams and around rocks, our spiritual journey is a series of twists, turns, and loops. Draw a curved line to symbolize your path, and on it sketch or write out the twists, turns, and memorable moments that have taken place so far. Alongside each moment, jot down what it meant for you and what it's taught you.

Where I am is much
more important
to me than
someone else's
ideas of where
I ought to be.

REFLECT: Have you ever acted from fear? As you're reflecting on this, consider that many emotions—like anger, resentment, jealousy, pride—are actually rooted in fear.

CENTER: Your intention or reason behind what you do is far more important than what you're doing or how you're doing it. How do you think making decisions motivated by fear affects you? If your actions were less motivated by fear, how might your life be different?

ACT: Get curious. For anything that you want to do today, pause and ask yourself: "Is this desire coming from a place of love inside me, or is this coming from emotional pain and fear inside me?" Write down what you discover about yourself from this process.

REFLECT: What are you chasing? What are you reaching for? What are you wanting more of?

CENTER: Often, the missing piece people are searching for to feel complete and truly happy isn't found externally; it's found within themselves. Pause, put your hand on your heart, and recognize the essence of wholeness within you that's been there all along.

ACT: Take your inner self on a date. With nothing missing and nothing to look for and chase, simply enjoy being with yourself.

"You cannot have a meaningful life without having spiritual self-reflection. Know who you are and why you are here. When you tap into that space, divine flow, that universal energy, you become untouchable in what you are called to do."

—**OPRAH WINFREY**

REFLECT: What is a situation in your life that's causing you to have an emotional reaction?

CENTER: In a difficult situation, it can be tempting to point the finger at the other person. Though it's probably true that they contributed to the difficulty of the situation, there is often little that can be gained by focusing only on their role in it. What can you gain from trading your focus on them for a focus on you?

ACT: Rather than focusing on changing others, consider that the circumstances of your life are always bringing up aspects of *you* that might need healing and loving attention. Pause and ask yourself, "Why is what happened bothering me so much?" and "Am I really responding to the present moment or to a buildup of similar situations in my past where I couldn't use my voice, acknowledge my hurt, share my feelings, or stand up for myself?" Feel and write your answers in the space below.

REFLECT: Think of something you're doing that you don't know if you should keep doing (e.g., being in a friendship or relationship with a specific person, working on a certain project, etc.). When you think about it, what does your mind say you should do?

CENTER: Your soul speaks the language of emotions. If something doesn't feel right, you don't have to do it, you don't have to accept it, and you don't have to be around it, even if parts of your mind say you should. If it does feel good, the reverse applies. How do you think it would be to know your personal truth by the way it feels without having to think about it?

ACT: Let the question "Does this feel right?" guide your day. Ask the question every chance you get and pay attention to your body's signals of alignment (e.g., expansion) or misalignment (e.g., contraction). At the end of the day, get curious about the situation you need guidance on and write about what your body's signals suggest about whether you should stay the course or shift direction.

REFLECT: Think back to a time when something you did negatively impacted a person more than you expected. Was your behavior coming from a place of love or fear, from kindness or hurt?

CENTER: When other people interact with you from a place of pain, you feel down and create ripples that lead other people to feel down. On the other hand, when you act from a place of love, others feel loved and go on to share that love. Close your eyes and envision a world where everything is interconnected and the energy coming toward you and emanating from you each day is the energy of love.

ACT: What if the only thing on your to-do list was to love? Choose a day to make it so. Then write about your experience here.

I take my time to find and live from the fullness of my being. No pace is too slow to come back to myself.

REFLECT: Is there an area of your life where you tend to pretend that you're more engaged, more interested, or happier than you actually are? How do you pretend?

CENTER: People sometimes lie about their feelings to come across as virtuous or likeable according to socially acceptable norms. Imagine you didn't have to do the things you're not interested or engaged in doing for the sake of appearances. How would you feel?

ACT: When you do something you don't really like or want to do, it's likely that a fear-driven part of you believes that you must. Bring to mind the area of your life in which you've been pretending, and ask yourself: "Why do I think that I *have to* do this? What am I afraid will happen if I don't?" As you listen inward for the answer, put your hand on your heart and offer yourself words of compassion like "This is so difficult" or "I'm so sorry you're scared."

"*All we are is peace, love, and wisdom, and the power to create the illusion that we are not.*"

—JACK PRANSKY

FINAL REFLECTION

Congratulations on taking a personal journey into your true self! Throughout this journey, you've done the courageous work of exploring what gives you meaning, who you really are, and how it feels to move in alignment with rather than against your true nature. Thankfully, the journey doesn't end here. The skills you've learned and the processes you've experienced in this book are yours to reuse, revisit, and repurpose to best suit the natural unfolding of your life.

I invite you to keep revisiting these questions as often as you need and to keep turning inward for answers. As you do, you'll notice that you inch closer to a life that is honest to you, that helps deepen your emotional awareness, that supports you in making choices that align with your truth, and that consistently honors your soul's greatest potential. You'll also recognize reminders that you are and have always been inherently worthy, and that there's absolutely nothing for you to prove and nothing to hide.

As the days and weeks go on, my hope is that you continue to see your truth, honor your preferences, and follow your heart. May you become the first place you go to for answers, wisdom, and love. May you love, dream, and hope in spite of your fears. And may you always know that you already are who you've always dreamed of becoming.

RESOURCES

The Awakened Brain

Book by award-winning researcher Lisa J. Miller, PhD, explores the science and power of spirituality.

PenguinRandomHouse.com/books/608347/the-awakened-brain-by-lisa-miller-phd

Caroline Myss

Programs and resources from influential spiritual teacher and renowned author Caroline Myss to support you on your path to becoming a more conscious, powerful, and aware person.

Myss.com

The Happiness Doctor Resources and Guides

Step-by-step guides, meditations, courses, and other intentional resources to support you along your journey of living a joyful, soul-led life.

TheHappinessDoctor.com/guides

The Happiness Hub Online Community

Online community devoted to learning, sharing, and building authenticity and joy among like-minded and like-hearted people.

TheHappinessDoctor.com/community

The Happiness Journal

A 52-week guided journal to develop genuine happiness—the by-product of a mindful and compassionate response to yourself and to life.

TheHappinessDoctor.com/the-happiness-journal

Neale Donald Walsch Online

Programs and videos from Neale Donald Walsch, author of the *Conversations with God* series of books, explore possibilities around God, life, and ways to express divinity in day-to-day life.

NealeDonaldWalsch.com

The Seat of the Soul Institute

Programs and tools to realize your soul's greatest potential from spiritual teacher Gary Zukav and his spiritual partner Linda Francis.

SeatOfTheSoul.com

Universal Human: Creating Authentic Power and the New Consciousness

Book from spiritual teacher and author of *The Seat of the Soul*, Gary Zukav, with tools for creating authentic power by aligning your personality and soul.

SimonAndSchuster.com/books/Universal-Human/Gary-Zukav/9781982169879

The Way of Integrity

Book from Martha Beck, a best-selling author and life coach, presenting a four-stage process for finding integrity and following internal signals that lead to your true path.

MarthaBeck.com/the-way-of-integrity

REFERENCES

Coelho, Paulo. "Maybe the Journey Isn't so Much about Becoming Someone. Maybe It's about Getting Rid of Everything That Isn't Really You #Hippie." Twitter. Twitter, June 24, 2018. https://twitter.com/paulocoelho/status/1010864837784690689.

Gilbert, E. (2006). Eat, Pray, Love: One Woman's Search for Everything across Italy, India and Indonesia. United States: Penguin Publishing Group.

Harris, Russ. ACT Made Simple: An Easy-to-Read Primer on Acceptance and Commitment Therapy. Cognitive Defusion Exercise. Oakland, CA: New Harbinger Publications, Inc., 2009.

Hesse, Hermann, Joseph Delage, and Jacques Brenner. Siddhartha. Paris: Grasset, 2017.

Lamott, Anne. "Let Us Commence." Salon. Salon.com, September 26, 2011. https://www.salon.com/2003/06/06/commencement/.

Merron, Keith. Inner Freedom: Living Authentically the Life You Were Truly Meant to Live. Tucson, AZ: Integral Publishers, 2013.

Moorjani, Anita. Dying to Be Me. Carlsbad, CA: Hay House, 2012.

Oprah Winfrey Delivers 2015 "Harry's Last Lecture" at Stanford University. YouTube. Stanford, 2015. https://www.youtube.com/watch?v=GR_7XOexvh8.

Singer, M. A. (2007). The Untethered Soul: The Journey Beyond Yourself. United Kingdom: New Harbinger Publications.

Turner, T. (2017). Belonging: Remembering Ourselves Home. United States: Toko-pa Turner.

Walsch, Neale Donald. The Complete Conversations with God an Uncommon Dialogue. New York: Tarcher Perigee, 2005.

Zukav, Gary. "Looking Back on Valentine's Day." The Seat of the Soul Institute, August 24, 2021. https://seatofthesoul.com/looking-back-on-valentines-day/.

ACKNOWLEDGMENTS

To all the wonderful people who give my life joy, love, and meaning and who provoke my spiritual growth and learning—my partner Joe DeLore, and my dear friends Tieg Alexander, Kristen Chazaud, Kristen Petrillo, Laura Khait, Illya Engle, Inna Breslin, Leo, and the Bershadsky family—I thank you from the bottom of my heart.

To everyone whose newfound presence in my life makes it one of increasing harmony, consciousness, and compassion—Laura Ratsch, Brian Sorrells, Kim Friedman, Jacque Fitzgerald, Paul Abodeely, Hart Haragutchi, Carla Duda, Martha Dodge, and my Internal Family Systems friends and colleagues—your openheartedness and soul-awareness continuously light the way for my own.

To Gary Zukav, Richard Schwartz, and all the amazing psychospiritual teachers who paved the way for a rising interest in self-healing and the ability to live a soul- and self-led life—I am truly and forever grateful.

To Brian Sweeting and the Callisto Media and Rockridge Press team, thank you for devoting your gifts to publishing works of meaning and purpose and for providing a space for my soul to express itself. I am delighted to co-create with you.

ABOUT THE AUTHOR

Sophia Godkin, PhD, is a health psychologist and happiness and healing coach best known for helping people cultivate genuine happiness and authenticity from the inside out. Better known as "The Happiness Doctor," Dr Sophia's work blends the principles and practices of positive psychology with therapeutic approaches to healing to make a holistic, inclusive, and heart-centered pathway to happiness possible. Whether in the form of individual and group coaching, courses, or writing, Dr. Sophia is known for the depth, light-heartedness, and transformative potential of her work. Visit her online and join her ever-growing community of people on their path to greater happiness at TheHappinessDoctor.com.